Cynthia Says Radio Show-Anger Is a Choice

What follows is a transcript from the "Cynthia Says Radio Show" It was broadcast in Shelton, Washington. There were nearly 30 shows in all. I started as a guest and became the co-host in this very fascinating series of discussions. This first discussion sets the tone and theme for the future shows.

This presentation is for educational and entertainment purposes. No therapeutic effect is intended or implied. If you suspect you have these issues please seek competent mental health counseling.

Cynthia and I have been colleagues for more than a decade and shared office space in our private practices. Occasionally we have worked together in group counseling or educational settings.

While I am no longer in counseling and have dedicated my time to writing and Life Coaching (Reality Lifestyle Observing), Cynthia continues to work as Life Coach and a Mental Health Counselor at her own private practice,

Griffin Counseling, LLC in Shelton and Lacey, Washington.

What we found is that we team together almost seamlessly. When she said that she was going to do a radio show, I jumped at the opportunity to work with her. The result was terrific.

After I had been writing for a year, she suggested that we do something together. So we had a transcript of one of our shows typed by James Harlan. After reading it, we decided that the form and content was so good we wanted to share it.

You will hear a professional partnership that is rare to find. It is born of mutual respect for our diverse personalities and skill sets.

You will notice that I am called J.J. in this segment. My name is James Nugent and my friends sometimes call me J.J. because my full name is James Joseph Nugent; Jr.

The ideas behind this discussion are somewhat based upon the ideas of William Glasser. He proposed that everything we do is an attempt to get our basic needs met. However, I have no idea if he would approve or disapprove of my interpretation of his theory of human behavior.

The show was fun and definitely an educational service to the small town of Shelton, Washington.

Welcome to Cynthia Says
Real World Issues, Need Real World Answers
We are here with your Host, Cynthia Dyrnes, a Licensed
Mental Health Counselor and Life Coach from Griffin
Counseling.

1) Cynthia's Introduction to Show
Cynthia: Our guest is JJ Nugent. Anger is our topic.
Healthy anger is a signal that something is wrong. It is a
signal that we have been hurt, that someone has crossed our
boundaries, that somebody has caused us pain. Anger is a
sign that we have experienced a loss or we have a fear of
losing something. What we do with anger is another thing.
How do we choose to express our anger? Do we express it
destructively by hurting another person or do we hurt
ourselves by turning it inward? That is also destructive.
What do you think about acting out with anger in ways that
hurt ourselves or others? Is that an ok thing to do? Well, it

4

is not. Let me tell you, it is a choice to act out in anger toward someone else. Make sure that you are acting as an adult and using your conscious mind to think about "what am I going to do with this emotion? Am I going to talk to the other person in a healthy manner, stating my feelings?" It is ok to be angry, but it is not ok to blast another person and blame them for your feeling of anger. Anger is an emotion that helps us move forward with our life. It tells us something about how we are interacting with our environment. If we are moving forward, then anger can be used in a positive, healthy way. There is something that we also call "Righteous Anger", which moves us to making a decision to protect ourselves or others.

Often it is because someone else is being abused, then righteous anger helps us to act appropriately to protect another person. For instance, children or the disabled who cannot protect themselves.

2nd Segment
Cynthia: JJ Nugent is our guest and we are talking about anger and emotional management through choice. JJ is a Certified School counselor and a step-father to two teenage boys. JJ what can you tell us about anger and the 5 basic needs?

JJ: Well Cynthia, when we anger, angering is actually an attempt to get what we want. Usually we are protecting 5 basic areas in our life. Perhaps it is basic survival issues like food, clothing, shelter, that sort of stuff or maybe it is quality of life like love and belonging, power, freedom, fun. Anyway, when we anger, when we feel that those needs are being threatened, we often get activated, we get angry, and we hopefully take responsible steps to get those needs met.

Cynthia: I heard you say angering like it is a verb. What is the origin of angering?

JJ: Well, we learn it as a baby and it is practiced throughout life, but think about it, an infant has no real way to communicate when they are cold, when they are hungry, when they are lonely, so what do they do? They scream, they anger, they tantrum. Hopefully, as they learn to communicate, they learn more sophisticated and more effective means of getting those needs met.

Cynthia: So as a baby, that is one of the ways we communicate through anger, through crying, through screaming…

JJ: Absolutely, one of the problems inherent in angering though is when that baby is crying, the parent has to guess. "Are they cold, are they hungry, are they lonely?"

Cynthia: Because it is not a direct verbal communication…

JJ: Right. It is definitely harmless in an infant.

Cynthia: It's expected!

JJ: It is expected and it is normal! One of the problems with anger is when a full grown adult tries to use anger to get their way.

Cynthia: Right, like in acting out and people who end up trying to control other people with their angry behavior…

JJ: Absolutely, and it is not all that effective. Yes, someone can throw a tantrum, destroy the house, make threats…

Cynthia: Throw dishes…

JJ: Sure and it could work for a little while, but we do have domestic violence laws and after awhile people will shy away from you, if you spend a lot of time angering, because it is scary.

Cynthia: The thing about the domestic violence laws these days is that even destroying property is considered domestic violence…or pulling the phone out of the wall so someone can't call for help or support. Even taking someone's keys or preventing them from leaving is considered domestic violence.

JJ: OH, absolutely, it is abusive! I am explaining anger but I am certainly not condoning angry behavior.

Cynthia: Well, and some of the other ways that angering looks like when people are acting out can be harassing others, trying to force your will upon others and get them to do what you want, and not stopping when someone says "NO" to you or "Leave me alone".

JJ: Yes, the roots of anger are that it is a selfish behavior and it is disrespecting the needs of other people. Again as an infant, as a child, even the terrible two's, it is normal to act out in anger until children learn more responsible ways.

But once you can reason and speak, it is not acceptable in any culture, I know, to try to force people to do what you want.

Cynthia: So JJ, are you saying that when grown adults act out with anger that they actually are throwing a temper tantrum like a two year old?

JJ: Sure, it is scary because they could do damage. Adults often hide that anger... oh they will try guilting out someone they are trying to coerce, threaten to harm themselves or harm someone else, cut themselves, that sort of thing. But again, it is a childish attempt to get what they want.

Cynthia: That is the ultimate temper tantrum! Threatening to hurt yourself to get someone else to do what you want them to do?

JJ: Sure, trying to actually make your victim feel guilty because they are not doing what you want them to do...

Cynthia: And that is also domestic violence if we threaten to hurt ourselves to get the person that we care about, that we are trying to control to do what we want. Threatening to hurt ourselves is against the law, it is domestic violence and it is something that we can go to jail for...

JJ: So Cynthia if anybody out there is caught in an abusive relationship like that they can get help by dialing 911 if they are in immediate danger, call your local crisis line, call your local domestic violence program, or even call child protective services, if children are involved. All of these resources can be found on the internet or in the phonebook.

Cynthia: The crisis line can also give you all of these local resources and give you information for private therapy so you can get support.

JJ: Yes, dealing with the victims of angering is something that counselors do well. I liked the way you started this radio show tonight with the idea that angering is a choice and there is a myth that we can be overcome by it. No, it's contrived and it can be a habit, and it can be a very comfortable habit. But that's not an excuse. It can be a very destructive habit! It's a lot more serious than chewing our finger nails. Think about it, at work, if you blow up, you lose your job. If you hurt someone in your house, you could leave in handcuffs. The habit of angering and acting out is absolutely destructive to the person acting out and also to the other people it is affecting!

Cynthia: And if we are stating that acting out in that way is a choice, then that means we have control over that behavior.

JJ: Oh sure, look at any child who is throwing a tantrum, it is goal oriented! "I want this, I want that". Just because you're six feet fall and 230lbs, if you're throwing a tantrum and you're busting up property and threatening to hurt people or anything like that, you're just doing what a three year old does.

Cynthia: That sounds dangerous.

JJ: Yes, very dangerous.

Cynthia: Now JJ, I'm going to switch gears here a minute and talk about an e-mail that came in after our last show. It fits in with what we're talking about. Last week we talked about the shadow and how the shadow can actually be manifested as angry tantrums, possessiveness, irrational behavior, overly emotional behavior and/or obsessiveness. It sounds like the shadow is a good news, bad news kind of deal. There are some good things about the shadow as well, it gives us signals and helps us survive in a threatening situation, but the question is, how do I integrate my shadow side with my light or higher self?

JJ: Wow! What a philosophical question! But, actually, anger is natural, it's normal and it serves a purpose. It really does provide for our survival and quality of life. If we pay attention to those angry signals we get, and say, what can I do right now in a constructive and responsible way to get these needs met? How can I collaborate with other people, not coerce, not try to force? How can I team and partner with someone else to get these needs met? That would be a mature and responsible adult point of view. It is important to realize that the way we are thinking directly affects the way we feel. So if we are thinking scary, angry, negative thoughts in any situation, then we are going to have those really powerful angry and unpleasant emotions.

Cynthia: To become aware of these negative emotions and the negative thoughts behind them is to become aware of our shadow or our survival mechanism or our survival strategies. It is actually bringing what is subconscious to the conscious level so that we have control over our actions. We have a quote from my producer who says "The choice to live demands that the truth be faced!" He is talking about denial there and when we are in denial, our shadow or survival stuff is in control. But if we make the conscious choice to recognize it and change our behavior, then we are coming into the truth. We are coming into integrating our shadow with the light.

JJ: Yes, it is hard to face that truth and often we don't want to face it with people we know socially and that is the perfect use for private counseling or life coaching, it is confidential and you can face the truth. There are parts of who you are that are natural and normal and have the potential to be destructive, and anger is one of them.

Cynthia: So JJ, I hear you saying that we do not have to be destructive with our anger to ourselves or others! We have the ability as rational human beings to become aware of our anger and make better choices for our futures. What kind of future do you want to create?

JJ: Yes, it really is our choice.

Cynthia: In fact, look around you, your present that you have created through your thoughts and actions surrounds you. What kind of a life do you want your future to look like? Think about the choices you are making right now...If you need some help with this stuff, then get yourself some counseling, some life coaching, talk to your pastor, your priest, your minister, your sports coach, your school counselor...there are all sorts of resources out there.

3rd Segment Last

Cynthia: Here is an email question that just came in: "Ever since I separated from my wife, I have felt elation! Every day I am anxious to return to my simple house where I feel great peace and joy. I also am wanting to start socializing with the opposite sex. Am I masking my grief with elation? What do I need to do to make sure I am not derailing my grieving process?" Sometimes grief can be expressed as other emotions, such as anger, especially for men in our culture. What can this person do to make sure they are not skipping the essential steps of the grieving process?

JJ: Well, I would be concerned if someone was experiencing only one major emotion after the loss of a marriage. You know, I think separation and divorce is so common in our culture now that we've forgotten or we don't admit how much it hurts. When we're hurt, One of the emotions that will come out is anger. And, I would say that this person who e-mailed in is very wise and they need to process that out. It's like losing an arm or a leg, I mean, it would be a very traumatic situation.

Cynthia: Well, the loss of a marriage would be a major loss. Its right up there with the biggies, like death of a spouse or child, sibling or parent. A divorce can feel like a mini death. It really is the death of a dream both partners share.

JJ: And it hits at all those basic needs, love and belonging, power, freedom, fun, even survival issues because it disrupts peoples' economic status. It sounds like this person is indicating (they use the word elation) that sounds like the 'fun' need to me. They have one of the basic needs being met, but I would be a little concerned that it's an unbalanced response. There's a richer deeper process for them to go through yet.

Cynthia: We just want to make sure that we're working on balancing the 5 basic needs... If fun starts to become like an escape behavior, we're actually diverting ourselves from our grief and loss over the loss of this relationship. That's when we get into trouble! Sometimes feeling the freedom and elation, if it goes to extremes we're masking our grief. A rule of thumb when we're moving on from a marriage or a significant relationship like that has been a long term relationship, take at least a year before you start dating or make any other important decision. Take the time to really process the emotions of that grief.

JJ: Then you will be freed up to relate fully with other people, and not have unresolved grief issues interfering...

Cynthia: It is extremely important to look at what happened in that relationship. What are the kinds of things we need to learn from what we have left behind? What were the patterns that occurred that we are in danger of repeating if we don't look at what happened? Definitely there is truth in the saying that 'History Repeats Itself"!

JJ: Sure, even if the spouse or partner was 98% the reason the relationship broke up. There is still the 2% of, for instance, why did you hang in a bad relationship for that long? Are there boundary issues, self esteem issues, co-dependence and fear issues that kept us stuck?

Cynthia: Good questions to ask ourselves. Let's look closely at our choices. Do we stay in relationships that aren't working? Do we stay longer then we should, than is good for us or our partners? Or our children? You know, addressing these things early and addressing them thoroughly with a counselor, with each other with direct communication is the best way to do it. But if it's not working folks, get yourselves out.

JJ: Another piece of that is, and this might sound cynical but, we go into relationships with high hopes and we look at all the positive things about the other person and how need fulfilling that other person is,

Cynthia: Right, that's why we get connected to people.

JJ: But it's like the tip of an ice berg… We also go into that relationship with all of our foibles and problems and quirks and dysfunctions and it feels normal and comfortable to us because we are used to them. So, we enter relationships with our own issues and we pair up with people who can tolerate, at least for a period of time those issues, and we need to look at our own issues before we inflict ourselves on somebody else.

Cynthia: Right…..we need to look at our shadow issues and what is at the core our responsibility, why this relationship was unsuccessful?

JJ: Sure, absolutely, and I believe in any relationship, it's give and take.

Cynthia: You do get to come in with a fresh start for a new relationship. However, that doesn't mean that some of these old things, the survival shadow stuff won't crop up, but you will be more prepared to deal with it and more equipped to come out with a better relationship for your future.

JJ: Well, I agree completely! The loss of a major relationship through death or separation is an opportunity to grow and become healthier and happier. So the person who wrote the e-mail, it's good that they feel elated, and I hope they continue to have those feelings, they just need to also face the other part of the relationship that they have a responsibility for creating.

Cynthia: Right, and it would be normal for any person who goes through this type of separation and loss of a significant relationship to feel sad. Experiencing those feelings of loss and even sometimes, depression would be totally normal. Now let's segue way back into how anger might fit in with this type of grief relationship, where grief is acted out as anger.

JJ: OK, as with any loss, I would expect someone to spend a goodly amount of time angry. Even if they don't think of themselves as an angry person, those emotions have to be dealt with. If they don't feel comfortable letting that anger out and experiencing that, well, then there's an issue right there that they need to work on, because emotions don't really go away they are just stored up and begin to leak out in ways that are inconvenient or destructive.

Cynthia: Destructive ways, for instance they can affect our physical health, our mental health, they affect those around us, our children, our other loved ones, our bosses, our co-workers, even our pets!

JJ: Yes, sure and one of the sad things we see spread throughout our communities is that so many people are medicating these feelings instead of facing the truth and experiencing these grief emotions and so they go to drinking and drugging and it just causes more misery for themselves and those around them.

Cynthia: What about angering as selfishness?

JJ: Because of its origins as babies and infants and toddlers, it is naturally selfish. We do turn inwards. Think about it....aha....I have a relative that almost refuses to look out the window when she drives. It is very dangerous for her to be driving around. That's really similar when a person is being angry and self centered. Their going through life making mistakes and blunders and potentially hurting other people because they are not thinking about other people, they're thinking about themselves.

Cynthia: So, it is like a horse at a race track with blinders on, they can see straight ahead of them but that's it. And, often if we don't see what's coming at from the side we're really missing out and ....ya.....It could be unsafe.

JJ: I saw a bumper sticker the other day and it said "there's no excuse for abuse" People use anger as an excuse or a explanation for all the things they do to other people.

Cynthia: Is there ever an exception to the rule JJ?

JJ: No.....no...I will use my car driving analogy, If I'm driving around and I run over somebody, its still manslaughter if they die.

Cynthia: That's right, you may still go to prison.

JJ: Ya....they don't call it murder, they call it manslaughter. It's an extreme example but we are still responsible for all the damage we do in the world. Damage can be physical, it can be emotional. Sometimes, I think some of the tragedies of angering or being habitually angry is that we deny other people the opportunity to relate to us because we are being so self-centered, other people don't really get to experience the good things that we have to offer.

This session ends and listeners are encouraged to seek competent mental health and spiritual counseling if they suspect that they have these or any other issues. This has been an educational discussion and no therapeutic benefits are prescribed or implied from participating or listening to this radio show.

End

Other Books by James Nugent

How I Sailed From Olympia to The San Juan Islands, and Returned Safely

An Alternative Boating Guide to Southern Puget Sound

How and Why I lived Aboard

Kayaking Budd Inlet in South Puget Sound

I Speak Esperanto

The Rainbow Road and Other Signs of God's Love

Living an Abundant Life, Within Your Means

Social Jujitsu and Powerful Principles for Managing Social Conflict

Blackjack on My Small Budget

A Little Benedictine Oblate Manuel

Without Speech

All things work

Loving Time with Your Creator

Personal Adventures in a Life of Learning

The Good News about Being Catholic

E-book Writing and Overcoming Barriers to Creativity

E-book Writing and Organizing Your Ideas

My Forty Days For Life 2013

Lifestyle Realty Observing

How to Sail in the Winter

How to Get Your Kid to Move Out

How to Get What Want (Hardcore Goal Setting and Achieving)

Sex, Abstinence, and Happiness

Available at Amazon.com in Kindle E-Book and or Audible Book or Paperback

Reflections and Notes

www.ingramcontent.com/pod-product-compliance
Lightning Source LLC
Chambersburg PA
CBHW070259300526
45791CB00022B/1666

* 9 7 8 1 4 9 4 8 5 3 2 1 1 *